THE LION IN THE FOREST

The Lion in the Forest

Kathleen McPhilemy

KATABASIS

First published October 2004 by KATABASIS
10 St Martin's Close, London NW1 0HR (020 7485 3830)
katabasis@katabasis.co.uk
www.katabasis.co.uk
Copyright © Kathleen McPhilemy 2004
Printed by CLE Print, Media House, Burrel Road, St Ives,
Huntingdon PE27 3LE (01480 465233)
Typeset in-house mainly in 12 point Garamond.
Front cover illustration: Ishtar Gate Lion, Babylon 6th century BC

ISBN 0 904872 40 8
Trade Distribution: Central Books
99 Wallis Road
London E9 5LN
(020 8986 4854)

British Library Cataloguing in Publication Data:
A catalogue record for this book is available
from the British Library.

ACKNOWLEDGMENTS

Some of these poems have appeared in *Acumen, HU, The London Magazine, The Rialto, Thumbscrew* and the anthology *In the Company of Poets* (Hearing Eye, 2003).

CONTENTS

I
Home   3
Door   8
Window   9
Walls   10
Roof   11
Floor   12
Secret Rooms   13
Confined Spirit   14
Afterwords   16
Mothers   17
Resonance and Wonder   18
Les Belles Dames sans Merci   20
Bits   21
Death of a White Horse   23
Hornlight   24
Snow   27
Redundancies   28
Failure of Imagination   29
GNVQ Student   30
Paying for Christmas   31
Change of Government   32
Losing the Plot   34
The Names of Flowers   35

II
Talking Politics   39
Collusion   40
The Twelfth of July, 1996   42
Swing   45
Closedown   46
Umbilical   47
Insomnia   48

Bad Blood   49
Winter Walking   53
That Deedlededeedlede Music   54
In the Clutch of Manannan   55

III
A Suite for Palestine   61
    Tallow
    Rosa, your Wound
    Instead of Stars
    Horn
    The Sandbed
    The Frown
    The Muffled Drum
    Knots
    Alien Blue
    Punishment Shootings
    Goodbye
    Why Irish?
    Communion
    Flower
Tenebrae Responsories   72
    Osculi me tradidit signo
    Intingit mecum manum in paropside
    Mittamus lignum in panem
    Quid dormitis?
    Tamquam ad latronem
    Sicut leo in silva
    Sequebatur eum a longe
    Hodie portas mortis
    Quomodo moritur iustus
    Signatum est monumentum

APPENDIX
Tenebrae Responsories:
Latin and English bilingual text   80

I

Home

'The foxes have holes and the birds of the air have nests; but the Son of man hath nowhere to lay his head.' – LUKE 9:57

1

You walk home, on an ordinary evening,
across the railway, up the lane,
but as you open the gate, a parked car
at the end of the road, beside the pub,
revs, starts up and drives away;
the picture slips, just a little,
like the missed step that jolts your dreams.

*

You want to go home, but it's late
and you're standing somewhere in a city
where the last door has closed
and only the street-lamps still shine.
A block or two to the east
there are voices and people talking
but you have forgotten which way is east,
forgotten where the sun will rise.

*

Someone is there; it may even be
someone you love who's there
and your home is suddenly
a house with rooms you can't be in.
Where you live,
as sure and unregarded as your skin,
becomes last year's sales mistake,
tacky and ill-fitting.
The place you called your own,

each little thing,
in someone else's pain,
turns ugly and is changed.

*

Home has left the house next door
and as if you'd had a stroke
that side of yourself has gone.
The window across the way
is black, dark as the wall
and night surrounding it.
You remember light on the stair,
the painting you never bothered to identify –
and people moving from room to room.

*

Where the heart is, where the hearth is,
home is where she is, but what she knows,
the heart is in the body and hers has changed so much.
From egg-head doll with tiny fingernails
through hefty girlhood to anorexic frailty;
ripe, tight as a plum, the bloom of babies
then earthward sag of cheek, upper arm
and folds of stomach: with every change of shape,
a change of heart till she understands herself
and knows that home is discontinuous.

2

When we arrived the place smiled at us,
English politeness we mistook for welcome
but a black cat came out under a barn door,
tail crooked high, and curved around our legs.
We fed it picnic scraps, dug the earth,
traced the pipes, measured walls and windows
and back in London, where anybody goes,
chose from a chart the paint for every room,
all shades of white, we wanted warmth and brightness.

*

In winter there was only the wind
that jerked the fire in the grate,
searching every gap and cranny
to vent its tuneless music.
The light-bulb above me flickered
and died in a soft explosion
but the plaster was wormy with voltage
and water flowed in the walls;
I was corded by pipe and cable.

Or in summer on a still night
under a matt sky, without stars,
when there were cattle out in the field,
through some freak condition of air
I could hear the sound of their breathing
magnified, all around me
till it seemed like the breath of the earth,
with me as the smallest particle
at the centre of the earth's breath.

*

All the place wanted was good husbandry,
it wanted to work, it wanted to be used;
we imagined new kitchens, barn conversions,
smallholdings, offices, thriving enterprise,
once even a whole village, ideal homes;
but without the money or the will, in high winds
slates flew off roofs, shattered, weren't replaced;
the great barn doors rusted from their hinges
toppling outwards to rot among the nettles.

We took the cat away with us, into the city.

3

'So he drove out the man; and he placed at the east of the garden of
Eden cherubims, and a flaming sword...' – GENESIS 3:24

Ashes over Fair Head
where land and water meet
let the winds decide
earth have no hold

fire at the cliff-edge
wills, contracts, title-deeds, treaties
thrown on the pyre:
all flags except
blank, white, wiped clean
a winding sheet.

Ash and smoke spiral
hang over the path
where the grey men fled
the abbey was burning
words up in smoke
choke gag speechless stifle.

At the change of the earth
a gentler fire
for the forge and the hearth
sword into wordshare

fair share shared space
heard over Fair Head
common words
common place.

Door

I have been knocked on many times.
I look both ways.
Like a horse or a hen
I have eyes in the side of my head.

She is dressed against the cold
but her hands are bare;
he will come down
in his moustache and long hair.

He will let her in.
She has come a long way
to this house
at the back of the North Wind.

Window

Why is she woman at the window?
Why does she watch the grass grow?
Who has come in behind her?
Does she not feel the draughts blow
under the door?

Woman staring through the glass
sees her chances pass her by.

She needs to get out.
This is not a place of safety.
A man might come into the house,
a man might come in with a gun –
and has done, many times.

If the door is blocked, climb out the window.
If the window is locked, break the glass.

Walls

As I see it, they are black and broken,
like bad teeth at the end of a life;
they do not now, allow for a roof,
stand against anything, keep out the cold.

Once, they held the windows in their grip,
fitted snugly round the door,
pipes and wires threaded through them,
water, gas, mysterious electricity;

inside, plaster, paper, paint
and picture hooks with pictures on them,
mirrors, bathroom tiles, plugs and switches,
fingerprints, marks of sticky hands.

Roof

Under the roof is where the cat goes
when it wants to die, where everything
we used to be has drifted, like shed skin,
upwards on the draughts that will come in
though we've locked the doors,
sealed the walls and windows.

I've climbed the ladder to cower in the loft
among the surfboards, sledges, discarded books,
the sheets of insulation flapping from the rafters;
closing my eyes, I wait in nervy darkness
for an ungentle giant hand to raise the roof.

Floor

I thought I had finished
but when I closed my eyes
I saw the flagstones, worn, flecked,
shining slightly with a bloom of damp
from the earth they were laid directly on.

Over lifetimes they have taken their shape
from the boots and shoes that walked in dirt
through the dairy and down to the cellar
where hams were cured, game was hung
and the water in winter was waist-high.

If you live in a house built over a spring,
is the floor more or less reliable?

Secret Rooms

were always in my head
with stairs I'd only sometimes dare
to climb by. Round and round

looking for the window
looking for a face at the window
for that possibility.

More windows than doors:
somewhere an extra space
false floors, thick walls, an attic

but another attic with no ladder,
no trapdoor, just the blank plaster
the blank eye of a porthole window.

Confined Spirit

'Her blacks crackle and drag.'– SYLVIA PLATH, 'The Edge' from *Ariel*

I read your books and go to bed
in a caulked building, sound, unchinked
but there are always more rooms than I counted this morning.
Though my house is built flat above ground
noise comes up at night from the cellar
stripes of light that threaten my tread.
Do I want to know what's under the floorboards?
Do I want to unlock the secret door?
Do I want to remember the nightmare of childhood
at the bottom of the pit with leprous bones?

Why must I take on your bad dreams?
Mouthy Medusa, Long John Silver,
names I walk by, museum pictures.
Should you be with them, emptied to flatness
or does your head still grin from the tree fork,
all skull and teeth through the hours of night?
Oh *bella donna,* I have dreamt you
your deadly nightshade, purple beauty;
you send your roots beneath my house,
forcing the concrete, splitting bricks and mortar.

Lend me your lantern, shady lady,
invisible slippers to creep downstairs,
follow the path of the dancing princesses
through fissured walls, under your roots
out to the starlight, music and laughter.

One wrong step and the walls close in
pulsing, warm, a red darkness,
terror cellar where murder's done,
under the floor limbs and tongues
buried, unspeakable amputations.

Words are for more than wrapping wounds,
private pearls round private pain;
you went down, down to your own roots
tore your devil foot from the floor's grip
dragged it into the light of language.
What courage to wrest those shapes from silence!
But your house is empty and the doors bang;
did you forget the art of conversation
go down too long, too deep, too often
till the trapdoor slammed and your earth was stopped?

Afterwords

'Intelligent women never have enough
milk,' she said, for comfort, but didn't mention
(showing a tact I didn't think she'd have)
till later, when both of ours were doing fine,
that her first child was a surviving twin.
Your poem moved me to remember this,
a tiny, swaddled grief. I thought again
touched by your words, their feathery tenderness,
how lives can cross, obliquely, just at the moment
when something's happened, and how what little's said
is not taken up or thought significant.
Long afterwards, when more is understood
you can turn to writing poems as a way
of saying what, then, you couldn't say.

Mothers

'No. Go away!' I screamed at my mother
as she entered my dream in late adolescence,
shadow hanging over me like the past or the future.

In my book mothers were the tough ones,
sensible, feet flat on the ground, earth
bound to the realms of the possible.

Mothers were moody: their monthly cycle
like regular verses that opened expansively
with ice-cream after school, treats, new clothes
but whose lines shortened at the end of the month
as tempers and housekeeping money dwindled.

Mothers were clever but didn't show it,
deferred to children's and husband's brilliance;
the ancient history of the books they'd read
concealed except for the occasional gloss,
the dazzling and sometimes deflating footnote.

Mothers changed their names to Martha:
in the book I read their hands were busy,
their words grew bitter, burned the tongue.

Mothers were durable, almost unbreakable;
crushed by a cow against the wall,
got up, carried on, so the story goes
a little more slowly, swallowing Veganin,
and watching the secret bruises yellow.

Resonance and Wonder

'I would have a sudden sense of the scale of the lives these women lived as I watched them dab at their eyes, or sit with their hands over their faces, their shoes wrinkled and turned inward toward one another, in a circle. The dimensions of that other world opened around me and my stomach contracted.' – SEAMUS DEANE, *Reading in the Dark*

Some stories are more important
than fact, truer than fiction.

Imagine the scale:
kitchens in Derry,
in Sicily, Poland, the New World
cabled to the universe.

How would you deny
the spiritual dimension?
How would you
equal it?

Back doors lead to back yards
backing onto each other:
coal shed, dustbins, an outside toilet;

but the front doors open onto the street:
at the end of the street is an ocean
as wide as thirst.

When the sun lays its red
carpet on the water
it is saying the local
is less than enough.

I need a story
to take me beyond myself;
I need to experience
resonance and wonder.

Les Belles Dames Sans Merci

All of us have phantoms in our head,
woulds and wishes that rob us of the present;
my dreams are peopled by my other selves
who've never lived, who die again with day.

Beautiful ladies, your pale faces reproach me,
the mirrors you hold are ghastly and merciless.
I have chosen the path that leads by the river
through the greens and browns of the lowland seasons.

But still I wake with memories of colour,
bright-sashed dresses in tightly-thronged rooms
in your magical palace, high on the mountain,
deep in the forest, dancing all night.

And still I imagine the field full of horses,
huffing at the gate, their grass-scented breath
in the gentlest hours of a summer evening:
bay, black and brown, dun and chestnut.

Bits

Over two hundred years
of carefully recorded lineage
pranced out of a television screen
ears pricked, towards the starting post.

'But isn't it cruel?' interrupted
my casual admiration
my instinctive feelings of pleasure
at such animal beauty and grace.
'Isn't it cruel?' deleted
proudly as anthropomorphic,
left me stuttering for words
of convincing repudiation.

Oh, you can see they enjoy it –
but my other voice enjoined:
As the fox enjoys the hunt?
As the bear enjoys his baiters?
As the carp with a hook in his mouth
enjoys the jerks and twists of his struggle?

As cruel as anything else.
The secret is not to resist;
obedience has its rewards.

I can remember unbroken ponies
tricked into taking the bit
champing, and flexing their necks;
I can remember the mysteries of bitting
from the simplest jointed snaffle
to the formal bit and bridoon
with its glittering, jingling curb chain:
instruments of coercion.

A bar of steel in the mouth
behind the teeth and over the tongue
forcing the lips' soft corners
into the wrinkled hint of a grin.
Now, when I look at horses
I see their tongues, the flecks of foam
and imagine the taste of metal.

Death of a White Horse

I wanted to go on to the next thing,
to write the poem after this,
avert my eyes from the stained horse blanket
and what lay under it:
a hoof, lips, a white ear
and blood, coming from somewhere.
This was no apocalypse
just the end of an old horse,
a humane destruction.
After the colic, some kind of paralysis;
she stood, front legs splayed, terrified of falling.
We wedged her up, dragged bales for her to lean on,
poured hot water on inert flesh,
massaged it dry with sacks and towels;
though we rubbed and rubbed, the skin stayed cold.
Yellow light shone on the wooden panels
and iron mangers of the Victorian stalls
we'd made a loosebox from. The cobbled floor
was deep in straw. We glowed with effort;
it was almost cosy, a contained disaster.
The vet came, small and sandy haired;
with a freckled arm he gave a little shove
and hope collapsed. We tried again
with strong men, ropes and pulleys,
but we recognised the end.
I didn't know, but yes, I should have known,
you mustn't put a stabled horse outside
until the frost has melted from the grass.
Where there are survivors,
they can blame or make excuses.

Hornlight – *Hornenlicht*

After Coagula *by Paul Celan*

To write one word
would resonate
across the century, across the different tongues;
or her 'lovely legato line'
assuage the rawness of rasped hearts.

Ark of the word my unworthiest I
but also live beneath the curve of horn
closer, lower than the arc of sky.

Colour like sunlight in old stone
on a late winter afternoon
or woven carpets, varnished pine
candles reflect in faceted crystal.

In the yard, the colt's torn knee
ripped flesh against black hair
hosepipe on it hour after hour
blood, cold water.

Dot-to-dot nearer than the stars.
Hard to find the dried up river bed
white with bones, in the squelch of March
mud that clings and puddled grass;

on television everything has died
baboons, impala, at last the crocodiles
except the few who wait it out in culverts
amoral, like lost manuscripts.
Not a time to mention guns
remembered in the silence that surrounds them.

Under the curve of horn is where we live
and through the gate of horn true visions come.

Caught in the act of taking off our shoes
perpetually on the threshold of the stars;
changing patterns we recognise
only by the lines we draw between them
configurations in which we are included.

Embarrassed by the bluntness of my fingers
and all the limitations that I am,
I fumble secretly among your words
ashamed I've dared to meddle in your order
but you raise me through the gate towards the real.

What's real is here, at the level of dogs and cattle
their dirt, their smells; worn grass, bare earth
ribbed by wheels going down to the river
and martins, early, four or six,
dipping and drinking in the water meadows.

*

Two sticks crossed, lashed, set on fire
a pile of branches, limbs, lumps of coal
flame dizzily around the central darkness
void at the edge of sleep words can't cover
unspeakable, it swallows meaning, order.

Laden with their deaths, they labour upwards
blood sweats to the ground, flesh is broken open;
they see the overprinted earth, bruised grass
the fag-ends by the kerb, no further, no higher.

*

We draw our patterns down here in the dirt
create the heavenly orders with sticks in sand.
Burnished metal of perhaps a car
or bombcase like a polished mirror of the night
reflects the fire we sit round telling stories.

Your words live on among our constellations
as you survive, though differently configured
among the genes and atoms that make us up.
As I've made you up so you talk to me
risen again from the dried bed of the river.

Snow

If you open your eyes before you turn
from everyday chores straightaway to sleep
there is light on the wall;
it falls through the window
through the gap in the curtain from the life outside:
if you open your eyes, there are white landscapes
beyond houses and hedges, towards the river,
under the moon.

There are places between road and railway
where only animals have been;
in the deepest thickets there are blackberries
not even the birds have reached;
all now are white, their unshaken branches
laden with snow.
Behind the houses, the canal is frozen and glittering;
the deserted meadow is ice,
not even phantoms are skating
from the Rainbow Bridge all the way to Wolvercote.

Redundancies

What has happened to the boys?
Young women with wide-awake eyes
come and go through opening doors;
they have such poise,
proud possessors of the actual world:
but what of the boys?

Cyber warriors, heroes of hyper-reality
earphone-sealed from the actual world
they slouch from school to the corner;
or, fit for nothing,
pump themselves up for a life without work.

Look at the boys:
woolly hats pulled down round their ears
warm the space where their butterfly brains
flitter and shift to the flick of a switch.

What is it destroys,
and when does it happen, the light in their eyes?
Nursery, puberty or the moment they see
their father with no job, their mother with two:
what have we done to the boys?

Failure of Imagination

Another hour ticked through; the boiler flares,
pipes expand and the house creaks towards morning.
As daylight builds behind the curtain,
the first bird, hesitant, spills into song.
Though I know he's too old to keep tabs on,
I listen all night for the key in the door.
My fears are unspecific, like the wailing siren,
ambulance or police, that screams past the end of the street.

By day, I feel a spurious security:
the postman with his red bike doesn't alarm me,
I hardly hear the planes that pass overhead;
the air smells fresh, the newsprint is dry and clean
as I read with angry pity of all those other
children scrabbling in the dust of their bombed-out lives.

GNVQ Student

My favourite terrorist
has beautiful brown eyes
and dark curling lashes
a girl would die for;

he wants to be a Sufi
but he wants to be rich
and drive a big Mercedes.
He gives me grief:

an under-achiever
but he can talk the talk.
Every Tuesday morning
he has a headache.

I thought of him
when I saw that child
the Americans have caught
on the Afghan border –

Hamsad bin Laden.
My favourite terrorist
is a little bit older:
sweet sixteen.

Now we have trained him
what shall we do with him?
Now we have taught him,
shown him his vocation.

Paying for Christmas

For all at Campsfield House

Monday morning, dark and wet:
December without Christmas is the dankest month.
(January's redeemed as a fresh start
so deep in winter the only way is spring.)
Christmas without money is the cruellest time,
dark and cold, for energy is cash,
light and heat to keep the baby safe.
Without the baby there is only December;
we need the safety of the curves' arrest,
the cradling arms, the manger hollowed out,
the parental promise of encircling light,
paid for somehow, that repeated moment.

The baby is the promise of itself,
just for a moment, of encircling arms,
of the ring of light we work to generate
that comprehends before and after darkness,
the outcast on the road whose only kindness
is nothing nearer than the curve of space.
Just for a moment the work that we have done
can make the baby glow, fine as a filament,
a covenant, defining our relation,
the work we owe, each to each on earth,
a promise to ourselves, in darkest time
that January will bring return of daylight.

Oxford, 1996

Change of Government

Talking and drinking wine in gardens
French windows open into, it seems we've seen
more people lately, been more sociable.
Others feel it too, smile in the street;
even in our street, between the big houses
people meet and smile. But nothing's changed.

We get up, go to work, hear people talking
as we haven't heard them for nearly twenty years,
people who live in houses in our streets
talking power talk. Everything has changed.
We have to redefine ourselves, decide
who we are again, and where our place is.

It isn't them, it's us, or people like us,
people we've studied with, or who've taught us;
taken down again, from whatever shelf,
blink a little, rubbing shiny elbows
We make the choices now, our friends are friends
of junior ministers and our voices carry.

But what about the people not like us,
the poor and mad and sick and bad and dirty
swept off our streets into the hug of silence?
They're the darkness we feel our voices carry over
as we sip our wine beside the first floor windows
that open on our streets and summer gardens.

That's where they are now, we've moved over;
the powerful can't be on the same side as the poor
however nice, like us, concerned or caring.
I don't feel easy, I don't feel part of We
and the muscles on my face are stiff from smiling.
I'm used to being outside, I want to prowl and snarl.

That's not true, either. I have a garden
with house attached, in comfort, just like us.
There are two views, one the shining lure
and the other half-built site of possibles;
through the window, behind the chattering voices
a roar of drills and mixers in the street.

Losing the Plot

When I visit the allotment now
I no longer see work in progress,
I see it as work abandoned.

Fragments – a strawberry paragraph
indecipherable, faded to brown;
leafless lines of raspberries
sprawling, unpruned, dead wood.

Halfway up the page
is a rhyming couplet of leeks
still neat, but etiolated,
enough for a pauper's soup.

The door of the shed's fallen off;
it gapes like an open mind,
cluttered with broken tools
and empty compost sacks –

things that might one day be useful
and a wheelbarrow to take them away in.

The Names of Flowers

With acknowledgement to GEOFFREY GRIGSON, *The Englishman's Flora*

At forty-eight I'm not too old to learn
the names of flowers; to find the cuckoo flower
just as the cuckoo cuckoos April into May.

Shepherd's Purse in Grigson's English Flora
is a mean little plant. He takes it personally
too much to heart its name of Mother's Heart:
seed-purse like a heart the little boy
breaks off, it cracks in two, another taunts,
'You broke your mother's heart'; the cruelty
of little boys sent away to school.
My father was (was Grigson?) and MacNeice;
something of them is pressed between these leaves.

Names in the vernacular; that's what weaves us in
to centuries of noticing the shapes
and scents of flowers, putting them to use:
ground ivy, ale hoof is inconspicuous
with green to purple leaves, lurking by the hedge;
an aromatic plant, once flavoured beer,
its flowers are trumpets, blue and small and silent;
or antirrhinums from the garden centre,
looked at closely, are snapping Chinese dragons.
Who saw it first? How was it handed on?

Why should I want to study all this stuff?
Is it, at forty-eight, a substitute
for everything I'm now too late to learn,
a metonym for areas of knowledge,
places never been to, desiderata?

A day the rain had spotted only briefly,
above the waves the sun had shown translucent,
I spotted it, single beside the path
its stripy tiger leaves, its spotted tongue,
but lost the right way back and cannot say
myself, exactly where it was I'd found it.
Later, on the beach, I said my names:
Fair Head, Cariguisnagh, Rathlin Island
and this time added stalky alexanders
to nodding marguerites, increase of knowledge.

Is naming knowledge and is knowledge power?
The meadow's full of different greeny stuffs
but I don't know their names until they flower
and then past flowering turn to fruit and seed
past my knowing, grow into their names.

I'm not too old to grow towards my name,
at forty-eight join them in the meadow
and speak the language, the common names of flowers.
There has to be a place of understanding
after which we can test the jargons.

Midsummer night the young were in the meadow,
decks and sound systems in the nature reserve;
their solid music pounded through the night
as they sat and danced around their separate fires.
In my dreams I heard a common language!
And at my gate this morning feverfew
tells this year's version of the end of June.
Expected by the walls of farms and cottage gardens
hard to get rid of, once it's taken hold,
the herbal aspirin that puts to flight
feverish dreams, and, like the cuckoo flower,
a common plant that's been around for ages.

II

Talking Politics

I sat at the table between them
as day receded from the garden
at the hour of early dusk.

I was silent; they were speaking:
there was only one story that night
and the way they told it was different.

They were men with powerful faces,
lines reinforced on their cheeks
by thirty years of unchanged opinions.

The room was full of obscurities
but light and dark waxed eloquent
on the strength of their polished convictions.

Collusion

The grass by the track is sparse,
the earth shows through,
brown and sticky as sludgy paint
or old blood. At the bridge
a woman waits for a dog sniffing at clumps,
the skeletons of last year's thistles.
The water is still and murky,
green and dark, like RUC uniforms.
There is a ground mist
so nothing at any distance
can be seen clearly.
It is January, late afternoon,
at the end of a century.

Elsewhere, earlier, parked cars
blocked the road, forming a circle.
Inside it, a man was dying.
For a quarter of an hour
they let no-one through:
long enough to die in.
For a quarter of a century
as the marked cars departed by unmarked roads
they have died in the circles of silence.
We have thrown our stone
into the centre of the dark green water.
The circles have spread
until the ripples lip at the riverbank.

There have been no floods this year;
though some of the channels and runnels have filled,
the river has kept to its banks
and many of the wild birds who are used
to spend their winters on the meadow,

disappointed,
must have flown on further.
But now the skies are black with rain
which will pour,
like an accumulation of grief, unstoppable
till the river rises and spills,
till the light changes
and the water's a different colour.

Oxford, 1997

The Twelfth of July, 1996

There wasn't a hint of orange
in Trafalgar Square this year,
not a toot on an Orange flute,
not a thump on a Lambeg drum
on the twelfth of July this year
and of all the coloured balloons
that rose to greet Mandela,
not a single one was orange.
There were lunch-hour Londoners,
tourists, press, the Brixton follow-on;
there were flags and tee-shirts, mobile phones,
black English schoolboys skipping school,
there were black and white South Africans
on the twelfth of July this year;
uneasy as a white South African
I was there.

I cheered a victory I hadn't won
and not the victories I've inherited –
Derry, the Boyne and now, Drumcree –
hard to claim with pride
dishonest to disown;
as I waited in the sun
for President Mandela
in the shadows of my mind
in the grey Garvaghey Road
the Orangemen were marching.

Can you hear the Lambeg drum
from away beyond the corner;
the toot of the Orange flute
drawing nearer and nearer?
Do you see the boy with the mace?

What prestidigitation
as he whirls it round behind his head,
under his arm, through his legs,
up and down his fingers.
King William on his horse
rides high on the Orange banner;
the men below, archaic as nuns,
wear bowler hats and sashes.
They march behind their bands,
as dour as Afrikaners,
as doomed as miners.

The tune they play is the land,
the stones they have shifted and raised
into houses, factories, cities.
In the last stages of petrifaction,
they have the masks of gargoyles,
the speech and accent of toads;
they are monsters defending a treasure
whose value they scarcely remember.

What were the Orangemen ever
but reactive, bullies and gangsters?
Nonconformist, Dissenter, Protestant
that's where the treasure is
locked in the names like a code
whose key is rusty, undusted:
names that gave freedom to thought,
that stood against Church and State
said no to the hierarchies;
nothing here coloured orange
nothing here that spells marching.

On the twelfth of July this year
crowds filled the Square;
they were casual, undisciplined, friendly,
no-one had marshalled or marched them;
there wasn't a hint of a drum
they had come of their own free will.

Swing

There was a swing
overlaid by repeated swings in stories
that rhymed us in a stomach-lurching lift
above the wall to see the all beyond.

What was beyond?

The bowling club next door,
Saturday night the big band sound;
and, on the other side, the Bad Girls' Home.

A higher swing to see the River Lagan
as far as Shaw's Bridge, or even further
flowing through the fields outside the city;
after, we heard dogs howling in the darkness
from the suburbs and on out in the country.

Closedown

Someone has turned off the television,
someone has turned off the radio;
but I can hear the clink of saucepans,
I can hear the tap still running.

Someone has turned off the gas,
someone has turned off the electricity;
but I still have a box of matches,
I have lit a dozen candles.

Someone has turned off the water,
someone has blown out the candles;
I can hear the guns outside,
I can hear the darkness breathing.

Umbilical

In memory of Martin O'Hagan

At two o'clock in the morning
the phone rang again;
the voice was drunk or distraught.

Yes, I told him, we know;
yes, we've already heard
and the voice went away.

He must have been on a mobile
he didn't know how to use:
he stopped, but the line stayed open.

Over or under the sea
across the billowing darkness
sounds of grief in a kitchen:

the clatter of cups of tea
a door that opened and closed
breathless sentences, half-spoken.

I tried to shout down the phone
I tried to break the connection;
I tried, but the line stayed open.

Insomnia

Cats screech in the dead hours
like the sound of a fingernail scraping
in an empty well.

There is no love in the darkness:
only the drink-fuelled
moment of need.

Moonlight on the wall
is a stage for angry shadows
gesticulating, beckoning.

The man gets up from the bed;
he goes where the gun is;
he feels its oiled weight.

And returns it to the drawer:
it is his forbidden promise
his locked-up possibility.

Bad Blood

In Memory of Rosemary Nelson

The elegies we write are for ourselves:
the dead don't need them.

I know there is blood
but to and fro on the pavement
backwards and forwards to work
I haven't got time.
The taste is there in my mouth
morning and evening
there in the red of the Cityline bus
there to remind me
in the glass of wine that I drink
and a day has gone by.

The blood is browner and older
like the red-brown brick of the houses
or the rust on the bike that wintered outside
whose wheels move stiffly and slowly
day after day.

Planting too late in the spring
so much I would do if I could:
I dig and the water wells up
darker and colder than blood.

Suddenly there was sunlight:
the roses in the garden were transfigured
red as the blood from a new-made wound
that beads the skin, fresh and glistening.
The sign I read was not her words
but the word of her death, a clear command.

When they buried her
the streets were full of faces
mourning one of their own;
while in the same town
others shrugged, a gesture
harsher than indifference.

You were one of those;
family man, farmer, rose-grower
custodian of secrets.
Your face is hooded on the screen
Your voice stutters and jumps
in electronic distortion;
but I know who you are
I know how close you are to me.

I have bought dried blood
from the garden centre
to feed the roses
which grow and blossom.
I have walked through your fields of roses
growing line after line
only for money.
How much have you told,
how much is better kept silent?

That little nervous laugh, that shrug
those bewildered eyes –
whatever you did
whatever you thought you knew
you never knew the half of it.

But you've learnt about pain
the truth of a life
pumping into the gutter
that might be your own
your wife, or your child,
look under your car,
check your locks,
be wary of strangers
more wary of friends,
who know where you are
and if they are smiling,
beware of their smiles.

*

Trust no-one.
She didn't trust me
but I understood
the need for distrust.

Chain-smoking, driven
pared to a filament
but with a kind of grace
she carried herself
as a brimming vessel
ready to be spilled
ready to be broken.

*

Neither wine nor roses
the taste of blood stays in the mouth,
taints the breath, poisons kisses;
spilt blood rears between us
like the smothering wall of the Red Sea.

Though blood lingers
in the tar of the road
in the earth beneath,
that was reality
that was the moment
of absolute doubt,
teaching distrust
of people and poetry.

Intelligence understands
the as if of metaphor
but grace behaves
as if there were trust.

Winter Walking

A shot was fired and the birds went up
then settled back amid festoons of ivy
that swathed the leafless, January trees.

I remembered a tale that he had told
how when a bomb went off, the pigeons flew
and reporters, hurrying to the highest window
to see the pigeons, knew where the bomb had been;
how he had once, reporting an explosion
in a car park, sat on the bonnet of a car
to make his notes, and only later learnt
an unexploded bomb was in that very car.

I remembered Othello and all the storytellers
who dazzled women with the newness of their tales:
walking back through the bright millennium morning
with blades of sunlight flashing from the ice,
walking back to the darkness of my house.

That Deedlededeedlede Music

I'm out of love with Ireland
but every morning when I wake
there she is beside me.

Like a long week's unwashed sheets
or carpets full of dust
she's warm and too familiar,

her coffee-rings have stained
every page I've been to,

she leaves her words about
to trip me everywhere
in English and in Gaelic

and all the time she hums
that deedlededeedlede music:

I want to go and live
somewhere clean and white and speechless
along the Antrim coast.

In the Clutch of Manannan

1

It's not the few hot days
which tweak and tug at the memory:
when children lay awake, sweltering
and grownups played tennis or fished
through the long, light evenings.

No, days that are endlessly blue
arrive like foreign visitors
enjoyed, here for the present,
shallow, unresonant.

But on turbulent days when the wind
churns up the air in the street,
when the sky comes to a rolling boil
of colour and cloud and light
I remember the taste of the sea
the place where the sun sets its line
between Rathlin and Kenbane Head.

Or a word and a phrase in a book
flipping through random pages
silver, North Sea – and I'm there
on the road that leads into Portrush
dazzled to tears by the breakers.

2

That's a place I must do without
except for memories or three-day visits
just short enough to recharge nostalgia;
just long enough to fire a village hall

or shoot a child: I hear it on the news
between Dunseverick and Kenbane castles,
disintegrating strongholds of squabbling tribes.
Now caravan parks are clustered on the headlands
where drunken boys chase and beat up strangers
whose voice or skin is wrong. Whoever says
the Irish aren't racist should recall
the centuries they've practised on each other;
should visit the market stall in Ballyclare
where loyalist and BNP regalia
are indistinguishable; should recollect
the volkish dreams of Eamon de Valera.

3

Nowhere stays as it was left:
a chunk of coastline falls,
they build new harbour walls.
Everything has its own trajectory
and the place you leave grows away from you.

Here the growth is mostly heritage:
cleaned up paths and tracks,
curly-lettered plaques.

Looking from my sister's panoramic window
I see Mananan's fist break through the water,
scribble of white on the left side of the bay;
and on the other is the Grey Man's Path,
cliff riven for the sea-god's convenience.

We nestle in the rediscovered legend
too gratefully – pre-Christian, threatens no-one.
Up on the hill the caravan lights are twinkling,
the night is young, the boys are gearing up
for the walk to town and its attendant choices.

III

A Suite for Palestine

This sequence of poems is based on images borrowed from the poems of Paul Celan. All my borrowings are based on the translations of Michael Hamburger and all quotations are taken from his translation: Poems of Paul Celan, Anvil Press, London, 1988. *Although my poems are in no way a translation, they are triangulated between Celan (Jewish but with German as his mother tongue), myself (Irish and British) and the conflict between Israeli and Palestinian in the Middle East. The figure of Rosa in the poem is Celan's Rosa Luxembourg, but also the little girl in the red coat in* Schindler's List *and finally, both the Palestinian terrorist and one of the Israeli teenagers she killed. Poems by Celan which have been used include, in order,* Talglicht, Coagula, Totenhemd, In Memoriam Paul Eluard, Eis, Eden, Die Irin, Irisch, Tenebrae, Tau *and* Blume.

Tallow

When you were burning so low
unlightly you remembered
the little horse in the forest
leaping from leaf to leaf;
or was it a unicorn
white and only
dancing on the teeth of darkness
before you learnt history?

*

They brought you up
hairy fathers of the forest
neither one thing nor the other
and you with them, not even...
your wheat was frost-bitten
you were blue and motherless.

It wasn't Jason, but Cadmus
who sowed dragon's teeth
that turned into soldiers,
and later to poems:
the glory that was Greece
in a different before.

*

Your condition is tallow
a necklace of fire
enough rope to hang yourself;
the mulch of the forest sprouts twiggy fingers
out of time, like snow in the desert;
from out of the storm, from under the sand
more dead hands scrabble:
shall these bones sing
render their light?

*

Blue sky, light cloud,
a poem like a weather forecast,
seashells and sand,
life before puberty
before gold, before greed,
before plunder, before rape.
Wave to Jason as he sails towards consciousness,
the burgeoning boy in his bud of a boat.

Rosa, your Wound

Oh, Rosa,

you were not admired unreservedly
and that young man, most wanted,
who stares from my newspaper,
even he will have his admirers.

I conjecture a wound,
unassimilated brilliance;
his anger translates to difficult energy,
twitching, as you did, the axis.

When the winners have decided
his page in the history books,
will there be anyone, I wonder,
to write him a poem?

Instead of Stars

Have you seen those girls who scratch themselves,
scratch themselves
till they have sores on their hands
they wear like stigmata?

Why would they choose to relinquish the stars
for a ceiling so low they bang their heads,
bang their heads:
self-hatred assuming the suffering of others.

Was this your prescient self-selection,
red-coated rose of guilt and blame?

Are they happy, those girls who bind on explosives
under their breasts, against their hearts?
Tainted wethers, culled from the flock,
monstrously mothers and children of death.

Horn

The colour of old teeth
in a tremulous smile
or of old bones or piano keys
or even the colour of the horns of buffalo
solid and comforting
somewhere in Romania.

If you could have borrowed a buffalo skin
to hide yourself in
with your dream as snug
as a nut in its shell
you could have escaped
like the girl in the fairy tale.

Beyond the gates of ivory
beyond the gates of horn
the dreamer awakens
where you are, where you are now.

The Sandbed

What else coagulates?
Viscous, mucoid, clumping the grains
into irregular shapes that disfigure the sandpit;

like that line of tanks in the desert war
filled with wasted, molten conscripts
staining the sand in their red-hot finality;

the park-keeper rakes over the sandpit
the wind sweeps the desert clean.

The butcher, wiping his fingers, changes his apron,
sprinkles fresh sawdust and smiles across
to his woman assistant who handles the cash
hygienically sealed in her glass kiosk.

The Frown

You have fallen into the fault
the grim crevasse of the frown;
you have forgiven the you of your innocence
the light-child;
knowing what you know now

how can you forgive yourself?
you who are the face of darkness;
your tanks roll into Ramallah
crushing honour under their tracks
crumbling the light in the stone.

The Muffled Drum

You who
you who listen to the screams
you have wakened
no light wind can soothe
no wrinkling breeze;

lord of the waste
underneath the slag heaps
underneath the mountains of ash
your heart still beats:

listen
listen to the screams you have wakened.

Knots

After you threw the first stone
and the glass fell in splinters around you
the eyes of your friends in the shards
regarded you gravely.

You blame a man
for the word he withheld;
the burden the tree bears
is the weight of his silence.

You had a rope
you knotted and knotted:
reticulations
to snare the darkness;

a net of words
to cradle his head;
unspeakable and unspoken
went into the grave.

After you drowned in the silence
who should we blame?
Who should have told the rope
knot by knot out of the unspeakable?

Now that the words are withheld
under cover of darkness
death in the snow has become
death in the sand.

Alien Blue

What words would you choose to lay in his grave
to weigh down his lids
to shutter his eyes
still so blue, so sad, so abstract –
so unmistakeably German;
would it surprise you to learn he was Jewish?
Jewish and German on his mother's side
but never at home in the language.

What words would you choose to write in the sand
to smother his tongue
to cover his face
his swarthy skin, his fine white teeth
his lips so red, still full of blood –
so unmistakeably Semite;
would it surprise you to learn he was Irish?

Irish and Arab on his mother's side
but never at home in the language.

What words would you choose to strew on his grave
what script would you pick for your hands to crumble
as dust on his hair, dulling his eyes
blueing his skin with the ashes of language?
Will you be surprised by the gentle strangers
who finger the ashes, sift the sand
who decipher his name
who find him his place?

Punishment Shootings

Icy cold,
the moon is in the reeds
the wind stops:
the boy has come;
he sees the round black eye
that saw what he has done
that presses the white flesh of his thigh.

Because we know the edge
so you see we see
how black blood is on snow
how black and fathomless
hot blood is on ice.

Goodbye

You long for land
but the Irish woman
who is not your mother
takes your hand in hers
which is mottled with poverty.

She reads you your lines
but you don't speak the language;
her porky fingers
grow round you and through you:

the sound you hear
is groundless, groundless
as she waves you away
faster and further

further than far
from the only place.

Why Irish?

Is this your Orient
your imaginary land
here in the Occident?

At least you asked
before you marched past the cornfields
to those little white cottages.

Did you imagine
they would throw open their doors
open their hearts
so you could dig yourself in?

Communion

From so many places
they came to the water
dark and undrinkable;
they crossed the water
shining, undrinkable
to the imagined land;

which was somewhere and real
white houses, olive groves
taken.

And gave them paper,
nation, flag, homeland,
gave them ashes.

The Lord broke the bread
it crumbled to sand
on the lips of the dead;
wound into and round
each is the other
the bread broke the Lord.

Under the ash heaps
under the rubble
lies the broken Lord.

Flower

For you, Lord
in the desert
a flower blooms;

all we ever asked for
was milk and honey,
not this, this difficult rose:

she sits in the cafe, sipping a milkshake;
she stands in the bedroom, dressed to kill:
suddenly, in the desert, it is raining petals
and all the water has turned to wine:

for no-one, for nothing, for you, Lord
their hair will never turn grey.

Wir haben getrunken, Herr.
Das Blut und das Bild, das im Blut war, Herr.

Tenebrae Responsories

The full bilingual text of the Tenebrae Responsories *can be found in the Appendix on page 80.*

A Sequence for Iraq

Osculi me tradidit signo

When the barbarians entered the city
there was little resistance;
they were welcomed with waves and kisses
as they came in with their tanks and their guns.
How could the people resist
their gum and their perfect teeth
their tanks and their guns?

After twenty-five years of darkness
the people were practised in waving;
at checkpoints all over the city
people exploded in kisses.

Bewildered, with only one language
the b-b-b-barbarian
responds in the words he knows
for father, for mother, for child –
better he had never been born.

*

Intingit mecum manum in paropside

Yesterday was before:

we sat together at table,
hand brushing hand

as we passed round the wine
dipped our bread in the dish.

Tonight there are two of us missing,
but still we must eat.

our eyes do not meet for we know
it could have been us, any one of us;

as we mumble the bread with our lips
we remember,
and drink the wine to forget.

*

Mittamus lignum in panem

Brought up to think themselves good –
they are the US cavalry
the ones who ride in in white hats
whose mission is the fixing of broken things –
they expect to be welcomed and loved,
find it hard to be bombing children
on a diet of ashes and sand.

The leaders admit it's untidy –
redemption comes at a price.
Out on a faraway hillside
a shepherd girl dies with her sheep.
The leaders are partial to prayer:
their words rise upwards like smoke
but the lamb is wood in their mouths.

*

Quid dormitis?

Not one hour, not one eye open!
What was there to wait for?
What was the point in watching?
One by one, the sets flickered off.

We marched, wrote letters, signed petitions;
we were tired, we needed to sleep,
we still had the morning to deal with:
one by one, we shuttered our windows

all night, while the beam of the laser
guided bombs to a faraway city.

Where was the failure of attention
delivered us to one eye rule?
Round, unlidded, pitiless
its gaze is unsleeping and deadly.

*

Tamquam ad latronem

Although I was foreign and different
you garlanded me, offered me kingdoms,
and if I lopped off the odd head,
you said I was foreign and different.

But when I got rich, you decided
I was much too foreign and different;
you came against me with weapons,
you beat me, took all that I had.

Now I am shivering on your doorstep
and you have me just how you want me,

will you teach me how to speak English?
Will you allow me to dwell among you?

*

Sicut leo in silva

As the lion is lost in the forest,
the dandelions are bright on the bank;
he is the trees and the spaces between
where the sunlight falls on his flank,
he is the colour of last year's leaves.

The dandelions dance with the lambs
and the grass is glossy and green,
but the lion is parched in the desert,
he has lost himself in the desert,
his pelt is the colour of sand.

At the hour when darkness is made
the desert is a forest of crosses,
the lion dies with the lambs;
though the dandelions are bright in the fields,
the lambs are butchered and lost.

*

Sequebatur eum a longe

We followed it all on television,
watched, but from a safe distance.
We can't understand the sorrow
of the people in the land of broken things.
There is a multiplication of Marys
weeping at the doors of the morgues.

The people had walked in darkness;
the light when it came was blinding:
who can understand their sorrow?
The people of the dolorous kingdom
must live where one eye rules,
where only one language is spoken.

There are children who have lost their parents,
their brothers, their sisters, their arms:
so much so intransigently broken.
The barbarians are bewildered with sorrow;
the brokenness of the dolorous kingdom
resists them, resists their technology.

*

Hodie portas mortis

They have been to hell and back
but death is not defeated.
Witness their harrowed faces
as they set out to hunt through the corpses
under the merciless Saturday sun.

The bodies are just as they fell,
just as dead, and flyblown already.
They do not expect resurrection
only the decency of burial
in the cool dark, underground.

The prison doors are burst open,
the doors of the banks and palaces,
statues and idols lie shattered;
but the hillside is stoppered with tombstones
like white and motionless sheep.

Quomodo moritur iustus

Who cares if a just man dies,
one, or several, or thousands?
Show us the corpse of the tyrant!
But the tyrant can change his face
and speak in a different language.

The prison doors have burst open
so murderers mingle with the innocent.
How would you know if someone was just?
Wrapped in their clothes and their language
they all look foreign and different.

Empire imposes a peace
that doesn't allow for difference;
where everyone learns to speak English:
you can count the searchers for freedom
among the dead, underground.

*

Signatum est monumentum

Across the mountains and hillsides
caves are sealed with boulders;
soldiers guard them.

In the land of the dead
different freedoms are stirring,
malign and insurgent.

The beech trees of April
strive towards sunlight,
their leaves unfolding and greening
in urgent photosynthesis.

Parasitic on their roots
the plants of the necropolis,
corpse flower, hell-root,[§]
also push upwards.

[§] Toothwort, broomrape.

APPENDIX

Tenebrae Responsories

*Tenebrae (Darkness) is the name given to the service of Matins and Lauds
in the Catholic Church for the three days before Easter: Maundy Thursday,
Good Friday, Holy Saturday, because the candles lighting the service are
gradually extinguished until it is completely dark. Responsories are a series
of verses and responses sung after the Lessons of Matins.*

Tenebrae for Maundy Thursday

1. *Amicus Meus*

Amicus meus osculi me tradidit signo:
Quem osculatus fuero, ipse est, tenete
eum: Hoc malum fecit signum, qui
per osculum adimplevit homicidium.
Infelix praetermisit pretium sanguinis,
et in fine laqueo se suspensit.

Bonum erat illi, si natus non fuisset
homo ille. Infelix praetermisit pretium
sanguinis, et in fine laqueo se
suspensit.

2. *Iudas Mercator Pessimus*

Iudas mercator pessimus osculo petiit
Dominum: Ille ut agnus innocens non
negavit Iudae osculum: Denariorum
numero Christum Iudaeis tradidit.

Melius illi erat, si natus non fuisset.
Denariorum numero Christum
Iudaeis tradidit.

3. *Unus ex Discipulis Meis*

Unus ex discipulis meis tradet me
hodie: Vae illi per quem tradar ego:
Melius illi erat, si natus non fuisset.

1.

The sign by which my friend betrayed
me was a kiss: Whom shall I kiss, that
is he: hold him fast: He who
committed murder by a kiss gave this
wicked sign. The unhappy wretch
returned the price of blood, and in the
end hanged himself.

It had been good for that man that he
had never been born. The unhappy
wretch returned the price of blood
and in the end hanged himself.

2.

The wicked merchant Judas sought
out the Lord with a kiss: He, like an
innocent lamb, refused not the kiss of
Judas: For a few coins he delivered
Christ to the Jews.

It had been better for him if he had
never been born. For a few coins he
delivered Christ to the Jews.

3.

One of my disciples will this day
betray me: Woe to him by whom I am
betrayed: It had been better for him if
he had never been born.

Qui intingit mecum manum in paropside, hic me traditurus est in manus peccatorum. Melius illi erat, si natus non fuisset.

He that dips his hand with me in the dish is the man that will deliver me into the hands of sinners. It had been better for him if he had never been born.

4. *Eram quasi Agnus*

Eram quasi agnus innocens: Ductus sum ad immolandum, et nesciebam: Consilium fecerunt inimici mei adversum me, dicentes: Venite, mittamus lignum in panem eius et eradamus eum de terra vivientium.

4.

I was like an innocent lamb: I was led to be sacrificed and I knew it not: My enemies conspired against me, saying: Come, let us put wood into his bread, and root him out of the land of the living.

Omnes inimici mei adversum me cogitabant mala mihi: Verbum iniquum mandaverunt adversum me, dicentes: Venite, mittamus lignum in panem eius et eradamus eum de terra vivientium.

All my enemies contrived mischief against me: They uttered evil speech against me, saying: Come, let us put wood into his bread, and root him out of the land of the living.

5. *Una Hora*

Una hora non potuistis vigilare mecum, qui exhortabamini mori pro me? Vel Judam non videtis, quomodo non dormit, sed festinat tradere me Iudaeis?

5.

Could you not watch one hour with me, you that were eager to die for me? Or do you not see Judas, how he sleeps not, but makes haste to betray me to the Jews?

Quid dormitis? Surgite, et orate, ne intretis in tentationem. Vel Judam non videtis, quomodo non dormit, sed festinat tradere me Iudaeis?

Why do you sleep? Arise and pray, lest you fall into temptation. Or do you not see Judas, how he sleeps not, but makes haste to betray me to the Jews?

6. *Seniores Populi*

Seniores populi consilium fecerunt, ut Iesum dolo tenerent, et occiderent: Cum gladiis et fustibus exierunt tamquam ad latronem.

6.

The elders of the people consulted together, how they might by some craft apprehend Jesus and kill him: They went out with swords and clubs as to a thief.

Collegerunt pontifices et pharisaei concilium: Ut Iesum dolo tenerent, et occiderent: Cum gladiis et fustibus exierunt tamquam ad latronem.

The priests and Pharisees held a council: How they might by some craft apprehend Jesus and kill him: They went out with swords and clubs as to a thief.

Tenebrae for Good Friday

7. Tamquam ad latronem

Tamquam ad latronem existis cum
gladiis et fustibus comprehendere me:
Quotidie apud vos eram in templo
docens, et non me tenuistis: Et ecce
flagellatum ducitis ad crucifigendum.

Cumque iniecissent manus in Iesum
et tenuissent eum, dixit ad eos:
Quotidie apud vos eram in templo
docens, et non me tenuistis: Et ecce
flagellatum ducitis ad crucifigendum.

8. Tenebrae Factae Sunt

Tenebrae factae sunt, dum
crucifixissent Iesum Iudaei: Et circa
horam nonam exclamavit Iesus voce
magna: Deus meus, ut quid me
dereliquisti? Et inclinato capite, emisit
spiritum.

Exclamans Iesus voce magna, ait:
Pater in manus tuas commendo
spiritum meum. Et inclinato capite,
emisit spiritum.

9. Animam Meam Dilectam

Animam meam dilectam tradidi in
manus iniquorum, et facta est mihi
haereditas mea sicut leo in silva: Dedit
contra me voces adversarius meus,
dicens: Congregamini, et properate ad
devorandum illum: Posuerunt me in
deserto solitudinis et luxit super me
omnis terra: Quia non est inventus
qui me agnosceret, et faceret bene.

7.

You are come out as it were to a thief
with swords and clubs to apprehend
me: I was daily with you teaching in
the temple and you laid not hands
upon me: Yet now you scourge me
and lead me to be crucified.

And when they laid hands on Jesus
and held him fast, he said to them: I
was daily with you teaching in the
temple and you laid not hands upon
me: Yet now you scourge me and lead
me to be crucified.

8.

There was darkness when the Jews
crucified Jesus: and about the ninth
hour Jesus cried out with a loud voice:
My God, why hast thou forsaken me?
And bowing his head, he gave up the
ghost.

Jesus, crying out with a loud voice,
said: Father, into thy hands I
commend my spirit. And bowing his
head, he gave up the ghost.

9.

I delivered the soul that I had loved
into the hands of the wicked and my
inheritance is become to me like a lion
in the forest: My adversary spoke out
against me, saying: Come together
and make haste to devour him: They
placed me in a solitary desert, and all
the earth mourned for me: Because
there was none that would know me
and do good to me.

Insurrexerunt in me viri absque misericordia, et non pepercerunt animae meae. Quia non est inventus qui me agnosceret, et faceret bene.

Men without mercy rose up against me, and they spared not my life. Because there was none that would know me and do good to me.

10. Tradiderunt Me
Tradiderunt me in manus impiorum, et inter iniquos proiecerunt me, et non pepercerunt animae meae: Congregati sunt adversum me fortes: Et sicut gigantes steterunt contra me.

10.
They delivered me into the hands of the impious, and cast me out amongst the wicked, and spared not my soul: The powerful gathered together against me: And like giants they stood against me.

Alieni insurrexerunt adversum me, et fortes quaesierunt animam meam: Et sicut gigantes steterunt contra me.

Strangers have risen up against me, and the mighty have sought after my soul: And like giants they stood against me.

11. Iesum Tradidit Impius
Iesum tradidit impius summis principibus sacerdotum et senioribus populi: Petrus autem sequebatur eum a longe, ut videret finem.

11.
The wicked man betrayed Jesus to the chief priests and elders of the people: But Peter followed him afar off, to see the end.

Adduxerunt autem eum ad Caipham principem sacerdotum, ubi scribae et pharisaei convenerant. Petrus autem sequebatur eum a longe, ut videret finem.

And they led him to Caiphas, the chief priest, where the scribes and Pharisees were met together. But Peter followed him afar off, to see the end.

12. Caligaverunt Oculi Mei
Caligaverunt oculi mei a fletu meo: Quia elongatus est a me, qui consolabatur me: Videte, omnes populi, si est dolor similis sicut dolor meus.

12.
My eyes became dim with weeping: For he is far from me that consoled me: See all ye people, if there be sorrow like my sorrow.

O vos omnes, qui transitis per viam, attendite et videte si est dolor similis sicut dolor meus.

O all ye that pass this way, attend and see if there be sorrow like my sorrow.

Tenebrae for Holy Saturday

13. Recessit Pastor Noster
Recessit pastor noster, fons aquae
vivae, ad cuius transitum sol
obscuratus est: Nam et ille captus est,
qui captivum tenebat primum
hominem: Hodie portas mortis et
seras pariter Salvator noster disrupit.

Destruxit quidem claustra inferni, et
subvertit potentias diaboli. Nam et ille
captus est, qui captivum tenebat
primum hominem: Hodie portas
mortis et seras pariter Salvator noster
disrupit.

14. O Vos Omnes
O vos omnes, qui transitis per viam,
attendite, et videte: Si est dolor similis
sicut dolor meus.

Attendite, universi populi, et videte
dolorem meum: Si est dolor similis
sicut dolor meus.

15. Ecce Quomodo Moritur
Ecce quomodo moritur iustus, et
nemo percipit corde: Et viri iusti
tolluntur, et nemo considerat: A facie
iniquitatis sublatus est iustus: Et erit
in pace memoria eius.

Tamquam agnus coram tondente se
obmutuit et non aperuit os suum: De
angustia, et de iudicio sublatus est. Et
erit in pace memoria eius.

13.
Our shepherd, the fount of living
water, is gone, at whose passing the
sun was darkened: For he is taken,
who took captive the first man: Today
our Saviour burst open both the gates
and bolts of death.

He destroyed the prisons of hell, and
overthrew the might of the devil. For
he is taken: Today our Saviour burst
open both the gates and bolts of
death.

14.
O all ye that pass by the way, attend
and see: If there be sorrow like my
sorrow.

Watch, all ye people, and see my
sorrow: If there be sorrow like my
sorrow.

15.
Behold how the just man dies, and no
one takes it to heart: And just men are
taken away, and no one cares about it:
The just man has been taken from the
face of iniquity: And his memory shall
be in peace.

He was mute as a lamb before the
shearer, and he opened not his mouth:
He was taken away from anguish and
from judgment. And his memory shall
be in peace.

16. Astiterunt Reges

Astiterunt reges terrae, et principes convenerunt in unum: Adversus Dominum, et adversus Christum eius.

Quare fremuerunt gentes, et populi meditati sunt inania? Adversus Dominum, et adversus Christum eius.

17. Aestimatus Sum

Aestimatus sum, cum descendentibus in lacum: Factus sum sicut homo sine adiutorio, inter mortuos liber.

Posuerunt me in lacu inferiori, in tenebrosis, et in umbra mortis. Factus sum sicut homo sine adiutorio, inter mortuos liber.

18. Sepulto Domino

Sepulto Domino, signatum est monumentum, volventes lapidem ad ostium monumenti: Ponentes milites, qui custodirent illum.

Accedentes principes sacerdotum ad Pilatum, petierunt illum. Ponentes milites, qui custodirent illum.

16.

The kings of the earth stood up, and the princes joined together: Against the Lord and against his Christ.

Why did the people rage, and the multitude think mad things? Against the Lord, and against his Christ.

17.

I am counted among those that go down to the depths: I am as a man without help, free among the dead.

They have laid me in the lower pit, in darkness, and in the shadow of death. I am as a man without help, free among the dead.

18.

When the Lord was buried, they sealed up the tomb, rolling the stone before the entrance to the sepulchre: Placing soldiers to guard it.

The chief priests went to Pilate and petitioned him. Placing soldiers to guard it.